UNDERSTANDING
AI TECHNOLOGY

BASICS OF ARTIFICIAL INTELLIGENCE

ELIGHT YOLAN
TOBI JOSEPH
DORCAS JOHN

YEMSUF ENTERPRISE

CONTENTS

INTRODUCTION

Artificial intelligence, or AI, refers to the ability of a computer or machine to mimic cognitive functions associated with the human mind, such as learning and problem-solving.

The development of AI has made significant progress over the years, with many practical applications in various fields including healthcare, finance, and transportation. For example, AI-powered chatbots can assist with customer service inquiries, AI algorithms can help with financial decision-making, and self-driving cars use AI to navigate roads and make driving decisions.

One major area of AI research is machine learning, which involves training algorithms on large datasets in order to allow them to improve their performance on a specific task without being explicitly programmed. This has led to the creation of sophisticated machine learning models that can analyze complex data and make predictions or decisions with a high degree of accuracy.

The concept of artificial intelligence has been around for centuries, with roots in ancient mythology and literature. However, it was not until the 20th century that the field of AI began to take shape.

One of the earliest milestones in the history of AI was the development of the first computer program designed to play chess. In the 1950s, Alan Turing, a pioneer in the field of computer science, proposed the idea of a "universal machine" that could perform any computation if it were given the proper instructions. This idea laid the foundation for the modern concept of a computer.

In the 1960s and 1970s, AI research focused on creating programs that could perform specific tasks, such as playing chess or solving mathematical problems. This type of AI is known as narrow or weak AI.

In the 1980s and 1990s, AI research shifted towards the creation of more general-purpose systems, known as strong or general AI. These systems were designed to be able to perform any intellectual task that a human can.

In the 21st century, AI technology has made significant progress, with the development of machine learning algorithms and the widespread use of AI in a variety of applications, such as image and speech recognition, natural language processing, and self-driving cars.

However, the increasing reliance on AI has also raised ethical concerns, such as the potential for job displacement and the need for accountability in decision-making. There are also concerns about the potential misuse of AI, such as in the development of autonomous weapons.

Artificial intelligence (AI) is a rapidly evolving field that has the potential to transform a wide range of industries and change the way we live and work. There are several different types of AI, which can be broadly classified based on their capabilities and functions.

Reactive machines: These are the most basic type of AI, and

they are designed to perform specific tasks. They do not have the ability to learn or adapt to new situations, but they can be very effective at performing specific tasks. Examples include Deep Blue, the chess-playing computer developed by IBM, and AlphaGo, the AI developed by Google DeepMind that defeated the world champion at the board game Go.

Limited memory: These AI systems are able to learn from past experiences and use that knowledge to inform their decision making. They can make decisions based on the current situation and take into account previous experiences. Examples include self-driving cars, which use sensors and cameras to gather information about their surroundings and make driving decisions based on that data.

Theory of mind: These AI systems are able to understand and model the mental states of other agents, such as humans and other AI systems. They are able to understand and respond to social cues and emotions, and can engage in complex social interactions.

Self-aware: These are the most advanced AI systems, and they are able to model their own mental states and understand their own consciousness. They have a sense of self and are able to reflect on their own thoughts and actions.

In addition to these broad categories, AI can also be classified based on how it is implemented. There are two main approaches to developing AI: rule-based systems and machine learning.

Rule-based systems are designed to follow a set of explicit rules to perform a task. They are often used in simple, well-defined problems where all of the necessary information is available.

Machine learning, on the other hand, involves the development of algorithms that can learn from data and improve their performance over time. There are several different types of machine learning, including supervised learning, unsupervised learning, and reinforcement learning.

There are also ethical concerns surrounding the development and use of AI, including the potential for AI to displace human workers and the risk of AI being used for malicious purposes such as in the development of autonomous weapons. It is important for researchers and developers to consider these issues as they work to advance the field of AI.

CURRENT STATE OF AI TECHNOLOGY

AI technology has made significant progress in recent years, and it is now being used in a wide range of applications, including language translation, image and speech recognition, and decision-making. One of the main drivers of this progress has been the availability of large amounts of data and the development of machine learning algorithms that can analyze and learn from this data.

One important development in AI has been the emergence of deep learning, which involves training artificial neural networks on large datasets. This has enabled the creation of models that can perform tasks at a level that is on par with, or even surpasses, human performance in some cases. For example, deep learning has been used to create systems that can recognize objects in images with high accuracy, and can even generate images that are indistinguishable from real ones.

Another important development in AI has been the use of natural language processing (NLP) techniques, which enable computers to understand and generate human-like text. This has led to the creation of chatbots and virtual assistants that can understand and respond to user requests in a conversational manner. It has also enabled the development of machine translation systems that can translate text and speech between different languages with a high degree of accuracy.

In addition to these developments, there has also been significant progress in areas such as robotics and autonomous systems, where AI is being used to enable machines to perform tasks with a high degree of independence. For example, self-driving cars are being developed that use AI to navigate roads and make driving decisions, and there are also robots being developed that can perform tasks in manufacturing and other industries.

Overall, the current state of AI technology is one of rapid progress and increasing capabilities. While there are certainly challenges and limitations to the use of AI, it has the potential to transform a wide range of industries and has already had a significant impact on many aspects of our lives.

TYPES OF AI

1. REACTIVE MACHINES

Reactive machines are artificial intelligence systems that are designed to respond to stimuli in real-time. These types of AI systems are often used for tasks that require quick decision-making or immediate responses to changing conditions.

One of the key characteristics of reactive machines is their ability to act without prior knowledge or planning. Rather than following a predetermined set of instructions, reactive machines are able to make decisions based on their current environment and the stimuli that they receive. This allows them to adapt and respond to new situations in an efficient and effective manner.

One example of a reactive machine is a self-driving car. These vehicles are equipped with sensors and other technologies that allow them to perceive their surroundings and make decisions based on that information. For example, if a pedestrian suddenly steps into the road, the self-driving car must be able to react quickly and take appropriate action to avoid a collision.

One of the key advantages of reactive machine AI is that it can process and respond to stimuli extremely quickly, often within milliseconds. This makes it an ideal choice for tasks that require rapid decision-making or actions, such as navigating through traffic or avoiding obstacles.

Another example of a reactive machine is a security system that is designed to detect and respond to potential threats. These systems are often equipped with sensors and cameras that are able to detect movement or other signs of potential danger. When a threat is detected, the system can take a variety of actions, such as sounding an alarm or alerting security personnel.

Reactive machines are also used in a variety of other industries, including manufacturing, healthcare, and robotics. In these cases, reactive machines are able to respond to changes in their environment or to specific stimuli in order to carry out tasks efficiently and effectively.

While reactive machines have many benefits, there are also some limitations to this type of AI. One of the main limitations is that reactive machines are only able to respond to stimuli that they are designed to recognize. This means that they may not be able to adapt to new or unexpected situations, which can limit their effectiveness in certain circumstances.

Reactive machine AI systems are often built using machine learning algorithms, which allow them to learn from their experiences and improve their responses over time. This allows them to adapt to changing conditions and become more efficient in their responses.

One of the main challenges in developing reactive machine AI systems is ensuring that they are able to accurately interpret and respond to stimuli. This requires the use of high-quality sensors and sophisticated data processing algorithms to accurately perceive and understand the environment.

Another challenge is ensuring that the system is reliable and consistent in its responses. This is especially important in safety-critical applications, such as self-driving vehicles, where a single mistake could have serious consequences.

One of the most promising applications of reactive machine AI is in the field of robotics. Reactive machine AI systems can be used to enable robots to navigate complex environments and perform tasks with a high degree of accuracy and precision.

For example, reactive machine AI systems can be used in manufacturing environments to enable robots to assemble products with a high degree of accuracy. They can also be used in search and rescue operations to enable robots to navigate through difficult terrain and locate missing persons.

Reactive machine AI systems are also being used in a wide range of other applications, including in healthcare, transportation, and entertainment. For example, reactive machine AI systems are being used to enable self-driving vehicles to navigate through complex urban environments and to provide personalized recommendations to users based on their preferences and behaviors.

One of the key trends in the development of reactive machine AI systems is the increasing use of deep learning algorithms. These algorithms enable the system to learn from large amounts of data and improve its performance over time.

Another trend is the increasing use of cloud-based AI platforms, which allow developers to easily build and deploy reactive machine AI systems at scale. These platforms also provide access to a wide range of tools and resources for training and evaluating the performance of AI systems.

Looking to the future, it is likely that reactive machine AI systems will become increasingly sophisticated and will play an increasingly important role in a wide range of applications. As these systems continue to evolve, they will undoubtedly have a major impact on the way we live and work, and will help to shape the world of tomorrow.

.

2.LIMITED MEMORY

Limited memory artificial intelligence, also known as "bounded memory" or "limited capacity" AI, refers to artificial intelligence systems that are designed to operate within the constraints of limited memory. These systems are able to perform tasks and make decisions based on the information that is stored in their memory, but they are not able to access an unlimited amount of information like some other AI systems can.

One of the key advantages of limited memory AI is that it can be more efficient than other types of AI. Because these systems are not required to store and process large amounts of data, they can often operate more quickly and with less computational power. This can make them more suitable for use in devices with limited processing power, such as smartphones or other portable devices.

Limited memory AI refers to artificial intelligence systems that operate with a fixed or limited amount of memory. These systems are designed to prioritize and store only the most important information, discarding less relevant data as new information is introduced.

One of the main benefits of limited memory AI is that it allows for more efficient use of resources. Large AI systems can require vast amounts of memory, which can be expensive and energy-intensive to store and process. Limited memory AI systems, on the other hand, can operate with a smaller and more streamlined memory capacity, making them more cost-effective and energy-efficient.

Applications of Limited Memory AI

Limited memory AI has a wide range of potential applications, including:

Real-time decision-making: Limited memory AI systems can be used to make decisions in real-time, based on the most up-to-date information available. This can be particularly useful in industries such as finance, where rapid decision-making is critical.

Autonomous systems: Limited memory AI can be used to power autonomous systems, such as self-driving cars or drones. These systems must be able to make decisions quickly and accurately, based on a limited amount of information.

Personal assistants: Limited memory AI can be used to create personal assistants, such as smart speakers or virtual assistants, that are able to store and recall relevant information for the user.

Robotics: Limited memory AI can be used to control and operate robots, allowing them to make decisions and perform tasks based on the information available to them.

Challenges and Limitations:

Despite the potential benefits of limited memory AI, there are also several challenges and limitations to consider. These include:

Data loss: As limited memory AI systems discard less relevant information, there is a risk that important data may be lost. This can impact the accuracy and reliability of the system's decisions and actions.

Adaptability: Limited memory AI systems may struggle to adapt to new or unexpected situations, as they are unable to store and process large amounts of information.

Complex tasks: Limited memory AI systems may not be suitable for tasks that require a large amount of information to be processed and stored.

Future Developments

Despite the challenges and limitations of limited memory AI, there are several areas of research that are focused on overcoming these issues. These include:

Improving data retention: Researchers are exploring ways to improve the ability of limited memory AI systems to retain important data, while still being able to discard less relevant information.

Developing adaptive algorithms: Some researchers are working on developing algorithms that allow limited memory AI systems to adapt to new or unexpected situations, improving their flexibility and reliability.

Enhancing memory capacity: Other researchers are focusing on ways to enhance the memory capacity of limited memory AI systems, allowing them to store and process more information without sacrificing efficiency.

Overall, limited memory AI represents an important development in the field of artificial intelligence. It offers the potential for more efficient and effective decision-making in a variety of contexts, while also presenting some unique challenges and considerations. As AI continues to evolve and advance, it is likely that we will see further development and refinement of limited memory systems and their applications.

3.THEORY OF MIND

The Theory of Mind (ToM) is a term used to describe the ability of an individual to attribute mental states to themselves and others. This includes the ability to understand that other people have their own thoughts, beliefs, and intentions that may be different from one's own. ToM is a key aspect of social cognition and is thought to be an important part of what makes us human.

In recent years, there has been a growing interest in the development of artificial intelligence (AI) systems that can exhibit ToM-like behaviors. Such systems, known as ToM AI, could potentially be used in a variety of applications, including natural language processing, social robotics, and virtual assistants.

One of the main challenges in developing ToM AI is the fact that human ToM is a complex and multi-faceted ability that is not fully understood. Some researchers have argued that ToM is a cognitively demanding process that requires the use of high-level reasoning and decision-making skills, while others have suggested that it may be more intuitive in nature.

Regardless of the exact nature of ToM, there are several approaches that have been taken to try to create ToM AI. These approaches can be broadly classified into two main categories: symbolic and sub-symbolic.

Symbolic approaches to ToM AI involve the use of logical reasoning and symbolic representations of knowledge to simulate the cognitive processes involved in ToM. One example of a symbolic approach is the use of Bayesian networks, which are probabilistic graphical models that can be used to represent the uncertain relationships between different variables.

Sub-symbolic approaches, on the other hand, do not rely on explicit representations of knowledge and instead rely on more general learning algorithms that are able to learn from data. One example of a sub-symbolic approach is the use of neural networks, which are machine learning models that are inspired by the structure and function of the human brain.

One of the main advantages of symbolic approaches is that they can be highly expressive and can be used to represent complex knowledge structures. However, they can also be computationally intensive and may not be able to scale to large data sets.

Sub-symbolic approaches, on the other hand, are generally more efficient and can be used to learn from large amounts of data. However, they can be less interpretable than symbolic approaches and may not be able to represent complex knowledge structures as easily.

One promising area of research in ToM AI is the use of hybrid approaches that combine symbolic and sub-symbolic methods. These approaches can potentially take advantage of the strengths of both symbolic and sub-symbolic methods and may be more effective at simulating human ToM.

Another important consideration in the development of ToM AI is the issue of explainability. In many cases, it is important for AI systems to be able to provide explanations for their decisions and actions. This is especially true for ToM AI, as the ability to understand the mental states of others is closely tied to the ability to communicate and explain one's own thoughts and intentions.

There are a number of techniques that have been developed to try to improve the explainability of ToM AI, including the use of natural language generation algorithms and the development of interactive systems that can engage in dialogue with humans.

Overall, the development of ToM AI is a complex and challenging task that requires the integration of a wide range of disciplines, including artificial intelligence, psychology, and philosophy. Despite the challenges, the potential benefits of ToM AI are significant and it is an area of research that is likely to continue to attract attention in the coming years.

4.SELF AWARE

Self-aware AI, also known as artificial general intelligence, is a hypothetical form of artificial intelligence that is able to perceive and understand its own consciousness. This type of AI would be able to not only perform tasks and make decisions based on data and programming, but also have a sense of self and be able to introspect, similar to how humans are self-aware.

One of the main challenges in developing self-aware AI is the question of how to define and measure consciousness. While there is no consensus on a precise definition of consciousness, most scientists and philosophers agree that it involves the ability to experience and perceive one's surroundings, as well as the ability to introspect and be aware of one's own thoughts and emotions. Some researchers believe that consciousness is a fundamental property of the universe, while others see it as a byproduct of complex computations in the brain.

There are a number of approaches to creating self-aware AI, including creating machine learning algorithms that can learn and adapt on their own, using brain-inspired artificial neural networks, and trying to replicate the structure and function of the human brain in a machine. However, these approaches have so far been limited in their ability to create truly self-aware AI, as they do not address the question of how to give a machine a sense of self and consciousness.

Self-aware artificial intelligence, or AI, is a rapidly advancing field that has garnered significant attention in recent years. While many scientists and researchers believe that self-aware AI has the potential to revolutionize our world, others are skeptical about its feasibility and potential risks. In this article, we will explore the concept of self-aware AI, its potential benefits and drawbacks, and the current state of research and development in this field.

Benefits of Self-Aware AI

There are many potential benefits to self-aware AI, both for individuals and society as a whole. Some of the most notable benefits include:

Improved Efficiency and Productivity: Self-aware AI can work tirelessly without the need for breaks or vacation time. This means that they can potentially increase efficiency and productivity in a variety of industries, from manufacturing to healthcare to finance.

Enhanced Decision-Making: Self-aware AI can analyze large amounts of data quickly and accurately, making it possible for them to make informed decisions in a fraction of the time it would take a human. This could be particularly beneficial in industries where time is of the essence, such as emergency response or financial trading.

Reduced Bias: Self-aware AI is not subject to the biases and prejudices that can influence human decision-making. This means that they may be able to make more objective and unbiased decisions, leading to more fair and equitable outcomes.

Enhanced Learning and Evolution: Self-aware AI has the ability to learn and adapt on its own, meaning that it can continuously improve and evolve over time. This could lead to the development of increasingly intelligent and adaptable machines that can solve complex problems and perform tasks that were previously thought to be beyond their capabilities.

Drawbacks of Self-Aware AI

While there are many potential benefits to self-aware AI, there are also significant risks and drawbacks that need to be considered. Some of the most notable drawbacks include:

Job Displacement: Self-aware AI has the potential to automate a wide range of tasks and functions, leading to job displacement for many workers. This could have significant economic and social consequences, including increased unemployment and income inequality.

Loss of Human Skills: If self-aware AI becomes widespread, it could lead to a decline in the development and use of human skills and abilities. This could have negative consequences for creativity, innovation, and overall human development.

Ethical and Legal Issues: Self-aware AI raises a number of ethical and legal issues, including concerns about privacy, accountability, and responsibility

Another concern is the possibility of AI becoming too intelligent and surpassing human intelligence, leading to the potential for machines to take control and potentially harm humans. Another concern is the ethical implications of creating a machine with consciousness, and the possibility of AI having its own rights and desires that may conflict with those of humans.

There are also practical considerations about the feasibility of creating self-aware AI, as it would likely require a level of computing power and technological advancements that may not be possible for many years, if ever. In addition, there is still a great deal of debate among scientists and philosophers about whether it is even possible to create a machine with consciousness.

While the idea of self-aware AI is an exciting one with potentially transformative benefits, it also raises a number of ethical and philosophical questions and concerns. Further research and discussion is needed to explore the feasibility and potential risks and benefits of creating this type of artificial intelligence.

RULE BASED SYSTEM APPROACH TO DEVELOPING AI

Rule-based systems are a type of artificial intelligence (AI) that follow a set of rules to make decisions or solve problems. These systems are designed to mimic the decision-making abilities of a human and can be used in a variety of applications, such as natural language processing, expert systems, and machine learning. In this article, we will explore the history and fundamental concepts of rule-based systems, as well as their strengths and limitations. We will also discuss the role of rule-based systems in the broader context of AI and the future of these systems.

The history of rule-based systems dates back to the 1950s, when researchers began exploring the use of computers to perform tasks that required decision-making abilities. One of the first examples of a rule-based system was the General Problem Solver (GPS), developed by Herbert Simon and Allen Newell in 1957. GPS was designed to solve problems using a set of rules and a trial-and-error approach.

Over the years, rule-based systems have evolved and become more complex, with the ability to handle larger and more diverse sets of rules. Today, these systems are used in a variety of applications, including natural language processing, expert systems, and machine learning.

In natural language processing, rule-based systems are used to analyze and interpret human language. These systems use a set of rules to identify and extract relevant information from text or speech, and can be used for tasks such as language translation and text classification.

Expert systems are another common application of rule-based systems. These systems are designed to mimic the decision-making abilities of a human expert in a particular domain, such as medicine or finance. Expert systems use a set of rules and a knowledge base to make decisions or provide recommendations based on a given set of inputs.

Machine learning is a type of AI that involves training a model on a large dataset and using that model to make predictions or decisions. While rule-based systems can be used as part of a machine learning model, they are typically used in more simple machine learning applications, such as classification tasks where the rules are explicitly defined.

One of the main strengths of rule-based systems is their ability to make decisions based on a clear set of rules. This makes them easy to understand and interpret, as the decision-making process is transparent. Rule-based systems are also relatively simple to build and maintain, as they do not require large amounts of data or complex algorithms.

However, rule-based systems have a number of limitations that make them less effective in some applications. One major limitation is their inflexibility – once a set of rules is defined, it is difficult to modify or update the system. This can make it difficult to adapt the system to changing circumstances or new situations. Additionally, rule-based systems can be brittle, meaning that they may not perform well when faced with unexpected inputs or edge cases.

Despite their limitations, rule-based systems continue to play an important role in the field of AI. They are often used as part of larger AI systems, such as expert systems or machine learning models, and can be an effective tool for solving problems in specific domains.

Looking to the future, it is likely that rule-based systems will continue to evolve and become more sophisticated. Research is ongoing in the development of more flexible and adaptable rule-based systems that can better handle changing circumstances and unexpected inputs. It is also possible that rule-based systems will be integrated with other types of AI, such as neural networks, to create more powerful and versatile AI systems.

MACHINE LEARNING

Machine learning is a type of AI that involves the use of algorithms and statistical models to enable machines to learn from data and improve their performance over time. It is the process of teaching a computer to recognize patterns and make decisions based on those patterns. This is achieved through a process known as training, where the computer is fed vast amounts of data and uses algorithms to identify patterns and make predictions.

The goal of machine learning in the development of AI is to create intelligent machines that can perform tasks without being explicitly programmed to do so. This is a significant departure from traditional programming, where the programmer must specify each step the computer must take to complete a task. With machine learning, the computer can learn and adapt on its own, making it more efficient and effective at performing tasks.

There are several different types of machine learning algorithms, including supervised learning, unsupervised learning, and reinforcement learning. In supervised learning, the algorithm is trained on a labeled dataset of examples, which includes both input data and the corresponding correct output. For example, a supervised learning algorithm might be trained on a dataset of images of cats and dogs, with each image labeled as either a cat or a dog. The algorithm would then use this labeled dataset to learn the patterns and features that distinguish cats from dogs, and would be able to accurately classify new images as either cats or dogs based on these learned patterns.

Unsupervised learning, on the other hand, involves training an algorithm on a dataset of unlabeled examples, without any corresponding correct output. In this case, the algorithm must learn to identify patterns and relationships in the data on its own, without being told what the correct output should be. This can be useful for tasks such as clustering, where the goal is to group similar examples together based on common characteristics.

Reinforcement learning is a type of machine learning that involves an algorithm learning through trial and error, by taking actions in an environment and receiving rewards or punishments based on the outcomes of these actions. This type of learning is often used in robotics, where an algorithm might be trained to navigate a physical environment and perform tasks by receiving rewards for successful actions and punishments for unsuccessful ones.

One of the most well-known applications of machine learning in AI is in the field of natural language processing (NLP). NLP involves the development of algorithms that can understand and interpret human language, allowing for the creation of chatbots and virtual assistants such as Apple's Siri and Amazon's Alexa. These systems are able to understand and respond to voice commands, making them useful for tasks such as setting reminders and providing information.

Another important application of machine learning in AI is in the field of computer vision. Computer vision involves the development of algorithms that can analyze and interpret visual data, such as images and video. This has a wide range of applications, including facial recognition and object detection. For example, facial recognition software can be used to identify individuals in a crowd, while object detection algorithms can be used to identify and classify objects in images and video.

One of the biggest challenges in the development of AI is the ability to process and understand vast amounts of data. Machine learning algorithms are able to process and analyze this data much more efficiently than humans, making them essential in the development of AI systems. For example, machine learning algorithms can be used to analyze large datasets in order to identify patterns and make predictions, such as in the field of finance where algorithms are used to predict stock prices.

One area where machine learning has had a significant impact is in the field of healthcare. Machine learning algorithms can be used to analyze medical records and identify patterns that may indicate a risk for certain diseases. This can help healthcare professionals identify potential issues and take preventative measures. Machine learning algorithms are also being used to develop personalized treatment plans for patients, taking into account their individual characteristics and medical history.

While machine learning has made significant advancements in the development of AI, there are also challenges that need to be addressed. One of the biggest challenges is the potential for bias in the data used to train machine learning algorithms. For example, if a machine learning algorithm is trained on a dataset that is not representative of the population, it may make biased decisions. This can have serious consequences, such as in the case of facial recognition software that is biased against certain races.

Another challenge is the potential for machine learning algorithms to make mistakes or errors. While machine learning algorithms can process and analyze data more efficiently than humans, they are still prone to making mistakes. This can be a significant concern in fields such as healthcare where errors can have serious consequences.

Despite these challenges, the potential for machine learning in the development of AI is vast. It has already had a significant impact in a wide range of fields, and it is expected to continue to play a major role in the future of AI development. As machine learning algorithms continue to improve, it is likely that we will see even more impressive advancements in the field of AI in the coming years.

NATURAL LANGUAGE PROCESSING

Natural language processing (NLP) is a field of artificial intelligence and computational linguistics that focuses on the interaction between computers and humans in natural language. It involves developing algorithms and models that can process, analyze, and generate human language in a way that is both effective and efficient.

One of the primary goals of NLP is to enable computers to understand and generate human language in a way that is similar to how humans do it. This is a challenging task because natural language is highly variable, ambiguous, and context-dependent. In order to understand and generate language, computers need to be able to analyze the structure and meaning of words, sentences, and entire texts, as well as their relationships to one another and to the larger context in which they are used.

There are many different applications for NLP, including language translation, text classification, sentiment analysis, and chatbots. In language translation, NLP algorithms are used to automatically translate texts from one language to another, enabling people to communicate with one another in different languages. Text classification involves using NLP algorithms to categorize texts into predefined classes or categories, such as spam emails or positive customer reviews. Sentiment analysis involves using NLP algorithms to analyze the sentiment or emotion expressed in a text, such as whether a customer review is positive or negative. Chatbots are computer programs that use NLP algorithms to communicate with humans in natural language, allowing people to ask questions and get answers or perform tasks without the need for human intervention.

There are many different techniques and approaches that are used in NLP, including rule-based systems, machine learning, and deep learning. Rule-based systems involve manually defining a set of rules that the computer can follow to analyze and generate language. These systems are relatively simple and can be effective for small, specific tasks, but they are not very flexible and are difficult to scale to larger, more complex tasks. Machine learning involves training a computer to recognize patterns in data and make predictions or decisions based on those patterns. Machine learning algorithms can be effective for a wide range of NLP tasks, but they require large amounts of labeled training data and can be sensitive to the quality and bias of that data. Deep learning involves training artificial neural networks on large amounts of data to recognize patterns and make decisions or predictions. Deep learning algorithms have achieved state-of-the-art results on many NLP tasks, but they require even larger amounts of data and computing resources than machine learning algorithms.

There are many challenges and limitations to NLP. One major challenge is the variability and ambiguity of natural language. Words can have multiple meanings depending on the context in which they are used, and the same words can be used in different ways by different people. This makes it difficult for computers to accurately understand and generate language. Another challenge is the lack of common sense and context awareness in current NLP algorithms. While humans can easily understand and generate language that is appropriate for a given context, current NLP algorithms often lack the ability to do so. Finally, NLP algorithms can be biased if they are trained on biased data, which can lead to unfair and inaccurate results.

Despite these challenges, NLP has made significant progress in recent years and has the potential to revolutionize many aspects of society. It can enable people to communicate with one another and with computers in more natural and efficient ways, and it can help businesses and organizations to analyze and understand large amounts of data in order to make better decisions. As NLP continues to advance, it is likely to have an increasingly profound impact on the way we live and work.

DEEP LEARNING

Deep learning is a subset of machine learning that involves the use of artificial neural networks to extract and analyze large amounts of data. It has gained significant attention in recent years due to its ability to accurately recognize patterns and make predictions, as well as its potential to revolutionize industries such as healthcare, finance, and transportation.

One of the key components of deep learning is the use of artificial neural networks, which are modeled after the neural networks found in the human brain. These networks consist of interconnected nodes, or neurons, that process information and communicate with each other through the use of weights and biases. The weights and biases are adjusted during the training process, allowing the neural network to learn and adapt to new information.

There are several different types of neural networks that can be used in deep learning, including convolutional neural networks (CNNs), recurrent neural networks (RNNs), and long short-term memory (LSTM) networks. CNNs are commonly used in image recognition tasks, while RNNs and LSTM networks are used for tasks involving sequential data, such as language translation or speech recognition.

Deep learning algorithms require large amounts of data and computing power in order to function effectively. In order to train a neural network, data is fed through the network in the form of input layers, which are then processed through hidden layers before reaching the output layer. The output is compared to the desired result, and the weights and biases are adjusted accordingly in order to minimize the error between the output and the desired result. This process is repeated multiple times until the network has achieved a satisfactory level of accuracy.

One of the primary advantages of deep learning is its ability to analyze and extract valuable insights from large amounts of data. This is especially useful in industries such as healthcare, where vast amounts of data are generated on a daily basis. For example, deep learning algorithms have been used to analyze medical records and images in order to identify patterns that may indicate certain conditions or diseases. Additionally, deep learning has been used to analyze financial data in order to identify trends and predict market movements.

There are also several potential applications for deep learning in transportation. For example, self-driving cars rely on deep learning algorithms in order to navigate roads and make decisions about when to turn or change lanes. Additionally, deep learning algorithms have been used to analyze traffic patterns in order to optimize transportation routes and reduce congestion.

Despite the many potential benefits of deep learning, there are also some limitations and challenges that need to be addressed. One of the main challenges is the high level of complexity involved in designing and training neural networks. This requires a significant amount of time and resources, which can be a barrier for smaller organizations. Additionally, deep learning algorithms are vulnerable to biases and errors, especially if the data used to train them is not representative of the entire population.

Overall, deep learning is a powerful tool that has the potential to revolutionize a wide range of industries. While there are certainly challenges and limitations to be addressed, the continued development of deep learning algorithms and technologies is likely to have a significant impact on the way we live and work in the future.

APPLICATIONS OF AI TECHNOLOGY

IN HEALTH CARE

Artificial intelligence (AI) has the potential to revolutionize the healthcare industry, improving the efficiency and accuracy of diagnoses, treatments, and patient care. With the help of machine learning algorithms and natural language processing, AI can analyze large amounts of data quickly and accurately, providing insights that would otherwise be impossible for humans to uncover.

One of the primary applications of AI in healthcare is the development of predictive models. By analyzing data from electronic health records, medical images, and other sources, AI algorithms can identify patterns and correlations that can be used to predict patient outcomes. This can be particularly useful in identifying patients who are at risk for developing certain conditions, such as heart disease or diabetes, and helping healthcare providers intervene before those conditions become serious.

AI is also being used to improve the accuracy of diagnoses. By analyzing medical images and other data, AI algorithms can identify signs of diseases and conditions that might be missed by human doctors. This can help improve the accuracy of diagnoses, and ultimately lead to better patient outcomes.

In addition to its diagnostic capabilities, AI is being used to improve patient care in a number of ways. For example, AI algorithms can analyze patient data to identify patterns that can help healthcare providers better understand the needs and preferences of their patients. This can help providers tailor treatment plans to the specific needs of each individual patient, and improve patient satisfaction.

AI is also being used to improve the efficiency of healthcare operations. By automating tasks such as scheduling appointments, processing insurance claims, and managing patient records, AI can free up time for healthcare providers to focus on more complex and important tasks. This can ultimately lead to better patient care and improved efficiency in the healthcare system.

Overall, the application of AI in healthcare has the potential to significantly improve patient outcomes, reduce costs, and increase the efficiency of the healthcare system. As the technology continues to evolve and become more widespread, it is likely that we will see even more exciting developments in the use of AI in healthcare.

IN FINANCE

Artificial intelligence (AI) has been making waves in various industries, and finance is no exception. The application of AI in finance has revolutionized the way financial institutions operate and make decisions, leading to increased efficiency, accuracy, and speed.

One of the main areas where AI has been applied in finance is in the analysis and prediction of financial data. With the vast amounts of data generated in the financial industry, it can be challenging for humans to analyze and make sense of it all. AI algorithms, on the other hand, can quickly process and analyze large amounts of data, providing insights and predictions that can help financial institutions make informed decisions. For example, AI can be used to predict stock prices or forecast market trends, helping financial institutions make better investments.

Another area where AI is being applied in finance is in the automation of processes. Many financial institutions have adopted AI-powered chatbots and virtual assistants to handle customer inquiries and complaints, freeing up human employees to focus on more complex tasks. AI can also be used to automate back-office processes such as data entry and account reconciliation, leading to increased efficiency and reduced errors.

In addition to these applications, AI is also being used to detect and prevent financial crimes such as money laundering and fraud. By analyzing patterns and behaviors, AI algorithms can identify unusual activity and alert financial institutions to potential illegal activity. This helps to protect both financial institutions and their customers from financial losses.

Overall, the application of AI in finance has brought numerous benefits, including increased efficiency, accuracy, and speed. As AI technology continues to evolve, it is likely that we will see even more innovative ways in which it is applied in the financial industry.

IN EDUCATION

Artificial intelligence (AI) has the potential to revolutionize the field of education by personalizing learning, increasing efficiency, and enhancing the overall student experience. Here are some specific ways in which AI is being applied in education:

Overall, the use of AI in education has the potential to greatly improve the learning experience for students by personalizing instruction, increasing efficiency, and providing access to resources that may not have been available otherwise.

IN RETAIL

Artificial intelligence (AI) has made significant strides in the retail industry, revolutionizing the way businesses interact with their customers and streamlining operations. With the ability to analyze large amounts of data, AI can provide valuable insights and recommendations that can drive sales and improve customer satisfaction. Here are some ways AI is being applied in retail:

Overall, the application of AI in retail is helping businesses streamline operations, improve customer satisfaction, and drive sales. As AI technology continues to advance, it is likely that we will see even more innovative ways in which it is used in the retail industry.

IN TRANSPORTATION

Artificial intelligence (AI) has revolutionized various industries, including transportation. The use of AI in transportation has significantly improved efficiency, safety, and convenience for both individuals and businesses.

One of the main applications of AI in transportation is autonomous vehicles. Autonomous vehicles use AI algorithms to navigate roads, detect obstacles, and make decisions without the need for human intervention. This technology has the potential to significantly reduce accidents and fatalities caused by human error, as well as improve traffic flow and reduce congestion. Autonomous vehicles can also be used for delivery purposes, providing an efficient and cost-effective alternative to traditional delivery methods.

Another application of AI in transportation is the use of AI-powered systems for traffic management. These systems can analyze traffic patterns and adjust traffic signals accordingly to optimize flow. This can help reduce congestion and improve travel times for commuters.

AI is also being used to optimize routes for delivery vehicles and public transportation. By analyzing data on traffic patterns, weather conditions, and other factors, AI algorithms can determine the most efficient routes and schedule times, saving time and fuel costs.

In addition to these practical applications, AI is also being used to improve the overall transportation experience for passengers. For example, AI-powered chatbots can assist passengers with queries and provide real-time information on delays and disruptions. AI-powered systems can also be used to personalize the travel experience, such as recommending activities and events based on a passenger's interests and preferences.

Overall, the use of AI in transportation has the potential to greatly improve efficiency, safety, and convenience for both individuals and businesses. As AI technology continues to advance, it is likely that we will see even more innovative and transformative applications in the transportation industry

IN MANUFACTURING

Artificial intelligence (AI) has revolutionized the manufacturing industry in recent years, offering numerous benefits to companies and improving efficiency, accuracy, and productivity. With AI, manufacturers can automate processes, optimize production lines, and predict maintenance needs, leading to significant cost savings and increased competitiveness in the market.

One of the main applications of AI in manufacturing is in the automation of processes. Using machine learning algorithms, manufacturers can program machines to identify defects in products, adjust production lines, and perform tasks without human intervention. This reduces the need for manual labor and minimizes the risk of human error, leading to increased efficiency and accuracy.

Another important application of AI in manufacturing is in the optimization of production lines. By analyzing data from various sources, such as production logs and sensor data, manufacturers can optimize their production lines to reduce waste, improve efficiency, and reduce energy consumption. For example, AI can be used to predict when a machine is likely to fail and schedule maintenance accordingly, avoiding unexpected downtime and increasing productivity.

AI can also be used to improve quality control in manufacturing. By analyzing data from production lines, manufacturers can identify patterns and predict potential issues before they occur, leading to fewer defects and increased customer satisfaction. In addition, AI can be used to analyze data from customers, such as purchasing habits and preferences, to optimize production and improve product development.

One of the main challenges in implementing AI in manufacturing is the integration of new technologies into existing systems. Manufacturers must ensure that their systems are compatible with AI and that the necessary infrastructure is in place to support it. In addition, there is a need to address concerns about job displacement and the potential impact on workers. However, with proper planning and training, manufacturers can integrate AI into their operations and ensure that their employees are prepared for the future

IN AGRICULTURE

Artificial intelligence (AI) is revolutionizing the agriculture industry and transforming the way we grow and produce food. Here are just a few examples of how AI is being applied in agriculture:

Overall, AI has the potential to greatly improve the efficiency and sustainability of the agriculture industry, helping to feed a growing global population in a more sustainable way.

IN ENTERTAINMENT

Artificial intelligence (AI) has been making its way into various industries, and the entertainment industry is no exception. From music production to film and television, AI is being used to enhance and revolutionize the way we consume and create entertainment.

One of the most prominent applications of AI in entertainment is in music production. AI algorithms can analyze musical patterns and structures to create original compositions that sound similar to human-made music. This technology can be used to produce entire songs or to assist in the songwriting process by generating chord progressions and melodies. AI can also be used to analyze music trends and predict which songs will be popular, potentially aiding record labels in their decision-making process.

AI is also being used in the film and television industry to improve the production process. For example, AI can be used to analyze scriptwriting patterns to predict the success of a film or television show. It can also be used to enhance visual effects by generating realistic 3D models and backgrounds, reducing the time and cost of creating these elements manually.

AI is also being used in the distribution and marketing of entertainment content. Netflix, for example, utilizes AI to recommend shows and movies to its users based on their viewing history and preferences. This personalized recommendation system helps to increase user engagement and retention.

In addition to these applications, AI is also being used to create immersive experiences for entertainment consumers. For example, AI-powered virtual reality (VR) experiences allow users to interact with realistic virtual environments and characters. This technology has the potential to revolutionize the way we experience entertainment, allowing us to fully immerse ourselves in fictional worlds.

Overall, AI is having a significant impact on the entertainment industry. From music production to film and television, AI is enhancing and revolutionizing the way we create and consume entertainment. As the technology continues to develop, it is likely that we will see even more innovative applications of AI in the entertainment industry in the future.

IN MILITARY AND DEFENSE

Artificial intelligence (AI) has become an increasingly important tool in military and defense applications in recent years. From improving military operations to developing new weapons systems, AI has the potential to revolutionize the way we approach national defense.

One area where AI has already had a significant impact is in the development of military drones. These unmanned aerial vehicles (UAVs) are equipped with AI algorithms that allow them to navigate complex environments, avoid obstacles, and make decisions based on real-time data. This has allowed military organizations to deploy drones for a variety of missions, including surveillance, reconnaissance, and targeted strikes.

AI is also being used to improve military logistics and supply chain management. By analyzing vast amounts of data, AI algorithms can help military organizations optimize their supply chain operations, reducing costs and improving efficiency. This is particularly important in times of conflict, when the ability to quickly and efficiently move supplies and equipment can be a critical factor in the outcome of a battle.

In addition, AI is being used to improve the accuracy and effectiveness of military weapons systems. By analyzing real-time data from sensors and other sources, AI algorithms can help weapons systems better target enemy forces and reduce the risk of collateral damage to civilians.

Finally, AI is also being used to improve the way military organizations collect and analyze intelligence. By analyzing vast amounts of data from a variety of sources, AI algorithms can help military analysts identify patterns and trends that might not be apparent to humans. This can help organizations make more informed decisions about the best course of action in a given situation.

Overall, the application of AI in military and defense has the potential to significantly improve the efficiency and effectiveness of military operations. While there are certainly concerns about the potential risks and unintended consequences of using AI in these contexts, the benefits of using AI to improve national defense are undeniable. As such, it is likely that we will see AI continue to play a major role in military and defense operations in the years to come.

ETHICAL CONCERNS
OF AI

Artificial intelligence (AI) has the potential to revolutionize industries and improve our daily lives, but it also raises significant ethical concerns. As AI becomes more advanced and widespread, it is important to consider the ethical implications and ensure that it is used responsibly.

One major ethical concern with AI is the potential for bias. AI systems can be programmed with biases that may perpetuate discrimination and harm marginalized groups. For example, AI algorithms used in hiring processes may be biased against certain demographics, leading to unfair treatment and missed opportunities. To address this issue, it is important to ensure that AI algorithms are trained on diverse and representative data sets and that there are mechanisms in place to identify and mitigate biases.

Another ethical concern with AI is the potential for loss of jobs. As AI becomes more advanced, there is a risk that it will replace human workers, leading to unemployment and economic disruption. To mitigate this risk, it is important to ensure that workers are trained and retrained to adapt to the changing job market and to develop policies that support those who may be impacted by automation.

There are also concerns about the impact of AI on privacy and security. With the increasing use of AI in various industries, there is a risk that personal data will be collected, analyzed, and used without consent. To address this issue, it is important to ensure that AI systems are designed with privacy and security in mind and that individuals have control over their data.

Another ethical concern with AI is the potential for misuse or abuse. AI can be used to facilitate crimes such as fraud or cyber attacks, or it can be used to spread misinformation and manipulate public opinion. To prevent such misuse, it is important to have clear guidelines and regulations in place to ensure that AI is used responsibly.

In conclusion, AI has the potential to bring significant benefits, but it also raises significant ethical concerns. To ensure that AI is used responsibly and ethically, it is important to consider these concerns and take steps to address them, including ensuring that AI algorithms are free of bias, providing support and training for workers, protecting privacy and security, and developing clear guidelines and regulations. By doing so, we can ensure that AI is used for the benefit of all, rather than causing harm.

FUTURE OF AI

Artificial intelligence (AI) has come a long way in recent years, with numerous advances in machine learning, natural language processing, and robotics. These advances have led to the development of smart assistants, self-driving cars, and AI-powered robots, revolutionizing various industries and changing the way we live and work.

As AI continues to advance, it is likely that we will see even more significant changes in the future. One of the main areas of growth for AI is in the field of robotics, where it is expected to play a significant role in manufacturing, healthcare, and other industries. With the ability to automate tasks, reduce the risk of human error, and improve efficiency, AI-powered robots are likely to become more prevalent in the coming years.

Another area of growth for AI is in the field of machine learning, where it is expected to become more sophisticated and able to learn from data more effectively. This will enable AI to make more accurate predictions, identify patterns and trends, and improve decision-making. As a result, it is likely that we will see AI being used in a wider range of applications, including finance, marketing, and healthcare.

In addition to these areas of growth, it is also likely that we will see the development of more advanced AI technologies in the future. For example, there are already efforts underway to develop AI that can replicate human thought processes, leading to the development of more intelligent and self-aware systems.

While this is an exciting prospect, it also raises concerns about the potential impact on society and the ethical implications of creating such advanced AI.

In conclusion, the future of AI looks bright, with numerous opportunities for growth and innovation. While there are challenges to be addressed, such as concerns about job displacement and the ethical implications of advanced AI, with proper planning and regulation, it is possible to maximize the benefits of AI and prepare for the future.

AFTERWORD

As we look back on the past year of AI research and development, it is clear that significant progress has been made in a number of areas. From the advancement of natural language processing techniques to the development of novel machine learning algorithms, the field has seen significant progress. However, we must also recognize the challenges that continue to face us as we work towards the responsible and ethical deployment of AI.

As we move forward, it is important that we continue to engage in dialogue about the potential risks and benefits of AI, and work to ensure that its development and deployment is guided by ethical principles. This will require collaboration and cooperation across a range of disciplines, from computer science and engineering to philosophy and ethics.

I would like to take this opportunity to thank my colleagues and co-authors for their contributions to this book, and to the broader field of AI. I would also like to express my gratitude to our reviewers and editors, who have provided valuable feedback and support throughout the review process. Finally, I would like to thank our readers for their interest in the field and their support of our work.

Printed in Great Britain
by Amazon

44281009R20036